New
POINT SYSTEM WEIGHT LOSS COOKBOOK
2025

Simple and Flavorful Recipes to Stay on Track for a Balanced and Healthier You Featuring Breakfast, Soup, Beverages, Vegetables, Beef, Full Color Photos and More

By

Dorothy J. Thomas

© **Copyright** 2024 Dorothy J. Thomas - All Rights Reserved.

No part of this publication may be reproduced, distributed, or transmitted in any form or by any means, including photocopying, recording, or other electronic or mechanical methods, without the prior written permission of the publisher, except in the case of brief quotations embodied in critical reviews and certain other noncommercial uses permitted by copyright law.

DISCLAIMER

The information provided in this " *New Point System Weight Loss Cookbook 2025*" is for general informational purposes only.

It is not intended as medical advice, diagnosis, or treatment. Always seek the advice of your physician or other qualified health provider with any questions you may have regarding a medical condition. The author and publisher of this book make no representations or warranties of any kind, express or implied, about the completeness, accuracy, reliability, suitability, or availability of the information contained within.

Any reliance you place on such information is strictly at your own risk.

The recipes and dietary recommendations in this book are not tailored to specific individual needs, and readers are encouraged to consult with a healthcare professional or registered dietitian for personalized advice.

The author and publisher disclaim any responsibility for any adverse effects resulting directly or indirectly from the use of the information provided in this book. The inclusion of specific products or brands does not imply endorsement.

While every effort has been made to ensure that the information in this book is accurate and up-to-date at the time of publication, medical knowledge is constantly evolving, and the author and publisher are not liable for any errors or omissions.

CONTENTS

INTRODUCTION	5
Understanding the New Point System	5
BREAKFAST	**8**
LUNCH	**15**
DINNER	**22**
Snacks & Light Bites	**29**
DESSERTS	**36**
BEVERAGES	**43**
SOUP	**50**
VEGETABLES	**57**
BEEF	**64**
PORK	**71**
CONCLUSION	78
Meal Planning and Prep	79

INTRODUCTION

Understanding the New Point System

The New Point System is designed to help you make healthier food choices while still enjoying the foods you love. By assigning points to different foods based on their nutritional value, the system encourages balanced eating and supports weight loss or maintenance. This section will guide you through the basics of the system, how to use it effectively, and tips for incorporating it into your daily routine.

How the Point System Works

1. **Assigning Points**
- *Nutritional Value:* Foods are assigned points based on their calorie content, fat, protein, fiber, and other nutritional factors. Generally, lower-calorie and higher-fiber foods have fewer points, while higher-calorie and lower-fiber foods have more points.
- *Serving Sizes:* Points are calculated per serving size. Understanding serving sizes is crucial to accurately tracking your intake.

2. **Daily Point Allowance**
- *Personalized Goals:* Your daily point allowance is personalized based on factors such as age, gender, weight, height, and activity level. The goal is to create a calorie deficit for weight loss while ensuring you get the necessary nutrients.
- *Tracking Your Points:* Keep track of your daily point intake to stay within your personalized allowance. Use a food diary or an app to simplify tracking.

3. **Food Categories and Points**
- *Zero-Point Foods:* Some foods, such as most vegetables and fruits, may have zero points. These foods are encouraged because they are low in calories and high in nutrients.
- *Low-Point Foods:* Foods with fewer points are usually lower in calories and fat, making them ideal for weight management. Examples include lean proteins and whole grains.
- *High-Point Foods:* Foods with more points are typically higher in calories and fats. While they can still be enjoyed, it's important to consume them in moderation.

Calculating Points

1. **Basic Formula**
   - *Points Calculation: The basic formula for calculating points involves considering the food's calories, fat, and fiber content. For example, foods high in fiber and low in fat will generally have fewer points.*

2. **Using a Point Calculator**
   - *Tools and Apps: Utilize point calculators or apps to make the process easier. Input the nutritional information, and the tool will calculate the points for you.*

Tips for Using the Point System

1. **Plan Your Meals**
   - *Meal Planning: Plan your meals and snacks around your point allowance. This helps ensure you're making healthy choices and staying within your daily goals.*
   - *Balanced Diet: Aim for a balanced diet that includes a variety of food groups. Incorporate lean proteins, whole grains, fruits, and vegetables.*

2. **Portion Control**
   - *Serving Sizes: Be mindful of portion sizes, as they directly impact the number of points you consume. Use measuring cups or a food scale to help with accuracy.*

3. **Mindful Eating**
   - *Enjoying Treats: It's okay to enjoy occasional treats. The key is to account for them in your point allowance and balance them with healthier choices.*

4. **Stay Flexible**
   - *Adapt and Adjust: If you find that you're not losing weight or feeling satisfied, adjust your point goals or consult with a nutritionist for personalized advice.*

Common Questions

1. **What if I Go Over My Points?**
   - *Strategies: If you exceed your point allowance, focus on making healthier choices the next day and increase physical activity to balance it out.*
2. **Can I Use the Point System for Special Diets?**
   - *Flexibility: The system can be adapted for various dietary needs (e.g., vegetarian, gluten-free). Just ensure you're meeting your nutritional needs while staying within your points.*

3. **How Do I Handle Dining Out?**
   - *Planning Ahead: Check restaurant menus in advance for point information or choose lower-point options. Many restaurants now provide nutritional information to help with this.*

1
BREAKFAST

Welcome to the breakfast chapter of the *New Point System Weight Loss Cookbook 2025*! Breakfast is more than just the first meal of the day—it's a vital opportunity to fuel your body, ignite your metabolism, and set a positive tone for the hours ahead. Here, we focus on balanced, nutrient-rich meals that adhere to our innovative point system, ensuring you can enjoy delicious options while staying on track with your weight loss goals.

In this chapter, you'll discover a variety of scrumptious breakfast recipes designed to keep you satisfied and energized. Each dish is carefully crafted to offer optimal nutrition while fitting seamlessly into your daily point allocation.

Breakfast is not just about eating; it's about making mindful choices that support your long-term health. We'll guide you through the principles of our point system and provide practical tips for making the most of your morning meals. With these recipes and strategies, you'll not only kickstart your day with vitality but also stay motivated on your journey towards a healthier you.

Let's get cooking and make breakfast the highlight of your day!

- Prep Time: 5 minutes
- Cooking Time: 0 minutes
- Total Time: 5 minutes
- Servings: 1
- Point Value: 3 points

BERRY POWER SMOOTHIE

1 cup mixed berries (fresh or frozen)
½ cup plain Greek yogurt
½ cup unsweetened almond milk
1 tablespoon chia seeds
1 teaspoon honey
½ cup spinach

Method:

1. **Blend Ingredients:** Combine all ingredients in a blender.
2. **Process:** Blend until smooth and creamy.
3. Serve: Pour into a glass and enjoy immediately.

- Prep Time: 10 minutes
- Cooking Time: 10 minutes
- Total Time: 20 minutes
- Servings: 1
- Point Value: 4 points

VEGGIE OMELET

2 large eggs
1/4 cup diced bell peppers
1/4 cup chopped spinach
1/4 cup sliced mushrooms
1/4 cup diced tomatoes
1/4 cup shredded low-fat cheese
1 teaspoon olive oil
Salt and pepper to taste

Method:

1. **Prep Vegetables:** Chop and prepare all vegetables.

2. **Cook Vegetables:** Heat olive oil in a non-stick skillet over medium heat. Sauté bell peppers, mushrooms, and spinach until tender, about 3-4 minutes.

3. **Prepare Eggs:** In a bowl, whisk eggs with salt and pepper. Pour eggs over the cooked vegetables in the skillet.

4. **Cook Omelet:** Cook until edges are set, then sprinkle cheese over one half. Fold the omelet and cook until fully set, about 2-3 minutes.

5. **Serve:** Slide onto a plate and enjoy immediately.

OVERNIGHT OATS WITH CHIA SEEDS

- Prep Time: 5 minutes
- Cooking Time: 0 minutes
- Total Time: 5 minutes (plus overnight chilling)
- Servings: 1
- Point Value: 4 points

½ cup rolled oats
1 tablespoon chia seeds
½ cup unsweetened almond milk
1/4 cup plain Greek yogurt
½ teaspoon vanilla extract
½ teaspoon honey or maple syrup (optional)
Fresh fruit for topping

Method:

1. **Combine Ingredients:** In a jar or container, mix rolled oats, chia seeds, almond milk, Greek yogurt, and vanilla extract.
2. **Sweeten (Optional):** Add honey or maple syrup if desired.
3. **Stir and Chill:** Stir well, cover, and refrigerate overnight.
4. **Serve:** In the morning, give the oats a good stir and top with fresh fruit before serving.

GREEK YOGURT PARFAIT WITH FRESH FRUIT

- Prep Time: 5 minutes
- Cooking Time: 0 minutes
- Total Time: 5 minutes
- Servings: 1
- Point Value: 3 points

1 cup plain Greek yogurt
½ cup mixed fresh fruit (berries, apple slices, etc.)
tablespoon granola
1 teaspoon honey (optional)
½ teaspoon chia seeds

Method:

1. Layer Yogurt: Spoon Greek yogurt into a bowl or parfait glass.
2. Add Fruit: Top with mixed fresh fruit.
3. Add Granola: Sprinkle granola over the fruit.
4. Sweeten (Optional): Drizzle with honey if desired.
5. Finish: Sprinkle with chia seeds for added texture.

AVOCADO TOAST WITH TOMATO AND BASIL

- Prep Time: 10 minutes
- Cooking Time: 0 minutes
- Total Time: 10 minutes
- Servings: 1
- Point Value: 5 points

1 slice whole-grain bread
½ ripe avocado
½ cup cherry tomatoes, halved
Fresh basil leaves
1 teaspoon olive oil
Salt and pepper to taste

Method:

1 Toast Bread: Toast the slice of whole-grain bread to your desired crispness.

2 Prepare Avocado: Mash the avocado with a fork and season with salt and pepper.

3 Assemble Toast: Spread the mashed avocado evenly over the toasted bread.

4 Top with Tomatoes: Arrange cherry tomato halves on top of the avocado.

5 Garnish: Drizzle with olive oil and garnish with fresh basil leaves.

6 Serve: Enjoy immediately.

2
LUNCH

Welcome to the Lunch Table of Wellness!

In the midst of a busy day, lunch should be more than just a quick refuel; it's an opportunity to nourish your body and keep your energy levels steady.

In the *New Point System Weight Loss Cookbook 2025*, we've crafted a variety of lunch recipes that are as satisfying as they are mindful of your wellness goals.

Each dish is designed to align with the new point system, ensuring that you can enjoy your meal without the worry of overindulgence.

From vibrant salads bursting with fresh flavors to hearty soups that comfort without the calories, these recipes will keep you full, focused, and on track with your weight loss journey.

Whether you're meal-prepping for the week or looking for a quick fix, our lunch options offer something for every palate and lifestyle.

Let's make lunchtime the highlight of your day—delicious, healthy, and perfectly balanced!

- Prep Time: 10 minutes
- Cooking Time: 15 minutes
- Total Time: 25 minutes
- Servings: 4
- Point Value: 4 points per serving

GRILLED CHICKEN SALAD WITH LEMON VINAIGRETTE

2 boneless, skinless chicken breasts (6 oz each)

4 cups mixed greens (arugula, spinach, etc.)
1 cup cherry tomatoes, halved
1 cucumber, sliced
1/4 cup red onion, thinly sliced
1 avocado, sliced
2 tbsp olive oil (divided)
Juice of 1 lemon
1 tsp Dijon mustard
Salt and pepper to taste

Method:

1. **Prepare the Chicken:** Season the chicken breasts with salt and pepper. Brush with 1 tbsp olive oil.
2. **Grill the Chicken:** Heat a grill or grill pan over medium heat. Cook the chicken for 6-7 minutes per side until fully cooked (internal temperature of 165°F). Let rest for 5 minutes before slicing.
3. **Make the Lemon Vinaigrette:** In a small bowl, whisk together the lemon juice, Dijon mustard, remaining 1 tbsp olive oil, salt, and pepper.
4. **Assemble the Salad:** In a large bowl, combine the mixed greens, cherry tomatoes, cucumber, red onion, and avocado. Top with sliced grilled chicken.
5. **Dress the Salad:** Drizzle the lemon vinaigrette over the salad and toss gently to coat.

QUINOA AND BLACK BEAN SALAD

- Prep Time: 15 minutes
- Cook Time: 20 minutes
- Total Time: 35 minutes
- Servings: 4
- Point Value: 6 points per serving

1 cup quinoa, rinsed
2 cups water
1 can (15 oz) black beans, drained and rinsed
1 cup cherry tomatoes, halved
1 small red onion, diced
½ cup corn kernels (fresh or frozen)
1 avocado, diced
1/4 cup fresh cilantro, chopped
2 tbsp olive oil
Juice of 1 lime
Salt and pepper to taste

Method:

1. Cook quinoa: In a medium saucepan, bring quinoa and water to a boil. Reduce heat, cover, and simmer for 15 minutes, or until water is absorbed. Fluff with a fork and let cool.
2. In a large bowl, combine cooked quinoa, black beans, tomatoes, red onion, and corn.
3. In a small bowl, whisk together olive oil, lime juice, salt, and pepper. Pour over the quinoa mixture and toss to combine.
4. Gently fold in diced avocado and chopped cilantro.
5. Serve immediately or refrigerate for later.

- Prep Time: 10 minutes
- Cooking Time: 10 minutes
- Total Time: 20 minutes
- Servings: 4
- Point Value: 5 points per serving

TURKEY AND AVOCADO LETTUCE WRAPS

1 lb. ground turkey (99% lean)
1 ripe avocado, diced
large lettuce leaves (Romaine or Butterhead)
1 small red onion, finely chopped
1 clove garlic, minced
1 tsp olive oil
1 tsp ground cumin
Salt and pepper to taste
Optional: salsa, lime wedges for garnish

Method:

1 Cook the Turkey: Heat olive oil in a skillet over medium heat. Add the minced garlic and chopped red onion, sauté until soft. Add the ground turkey, season with cumin, salt, and pepper, and cook until browned, about 8-10 minutes.

2 Assemble the Wraps: Lay out lettuce leaves on a clean surface. Evenly distribute the cooked turkey across the leaves.

3 Add Toppings: Top each lettuce wrap with diced avocado and any optional garnishes like salsa or lime juice.

4 Serve: Roll up the lettuce leaves to form wraps and serve immediately.

- Prep Time: 10 minutes
- Cooking Time: 20 minutes
- Total Time: 30 minutes
- Servings: 4
- Point Value: 4 points per serving

SPINACH AND FETA STUFFED PORTOBELLO MUSHROOMS

large Portobello mushrooms
2 cups fresh spinach, chopped
½ cup feta cheese, crumbled (reduced-fat)
1 small onion, finely chopped
1 clove garlic, minced
1 tablespoon olive oil
Salt and pepper to taste

Method:

1. **Preheat Oven:** Preheat the oven to 375°F (190°C).
2. **Prepare Mushrooms:** Clean Portobello mushrooms and remove stems. Brush the caps with olive oil and place them on a baking sheet, gill side up.
3. **Cook Spinach:** In a pan, heat a teaspoon of olive oil over medium heat. Sauté onion until soft, add garlic, and cook for another minute. Add spinach and cook until wilted. Remove from heat and stir in feta cheese.
4. **Stuff Mushrooms:** Evenly divide the spinach mixture among the mushroom caps, seasoning with salt and pepper.
5. **Bake:** Bake for 15-20 minutes until mushrooms are tender and the filling is heated through.

- Prep Time: 10 minutes
- Cook Time: 30 minutes
- Total Time: 40 minutes
- Servings: 4
- Point Value: 2 points per serving

TOMATO BASIL SOUP

1 tablespoon olive oil
1 medium onion, chopped
2 cloves garlic, minced
1 (28 oz) can of crushed tomatoes
2 cups vegetable broth (low sodium)
1/4 cup fresh basil leaves, chopped
1/2 teaspoon salt
1/4 teaspoon black pepper

Method:

1   Sauté Aromatics: In a large pot, heat olive oil over medium heat. Add chopped onion and garlic, and sauté until softened, about 5 minutes.

2   Simmer Soup: Add crushed tomatoes and vegetable broth to the pot. Bring to a boil, then reduce heat and let simmer for 20 minutes.

3   Blend and Season: Stir in fresh basil, salt, and pepper. Use an immersion blender to puree the soup until smooth.

4   Serve: Ladle the soup into bowls and garnish with additional basil if desired. Enjoy hot.

3
DINNER

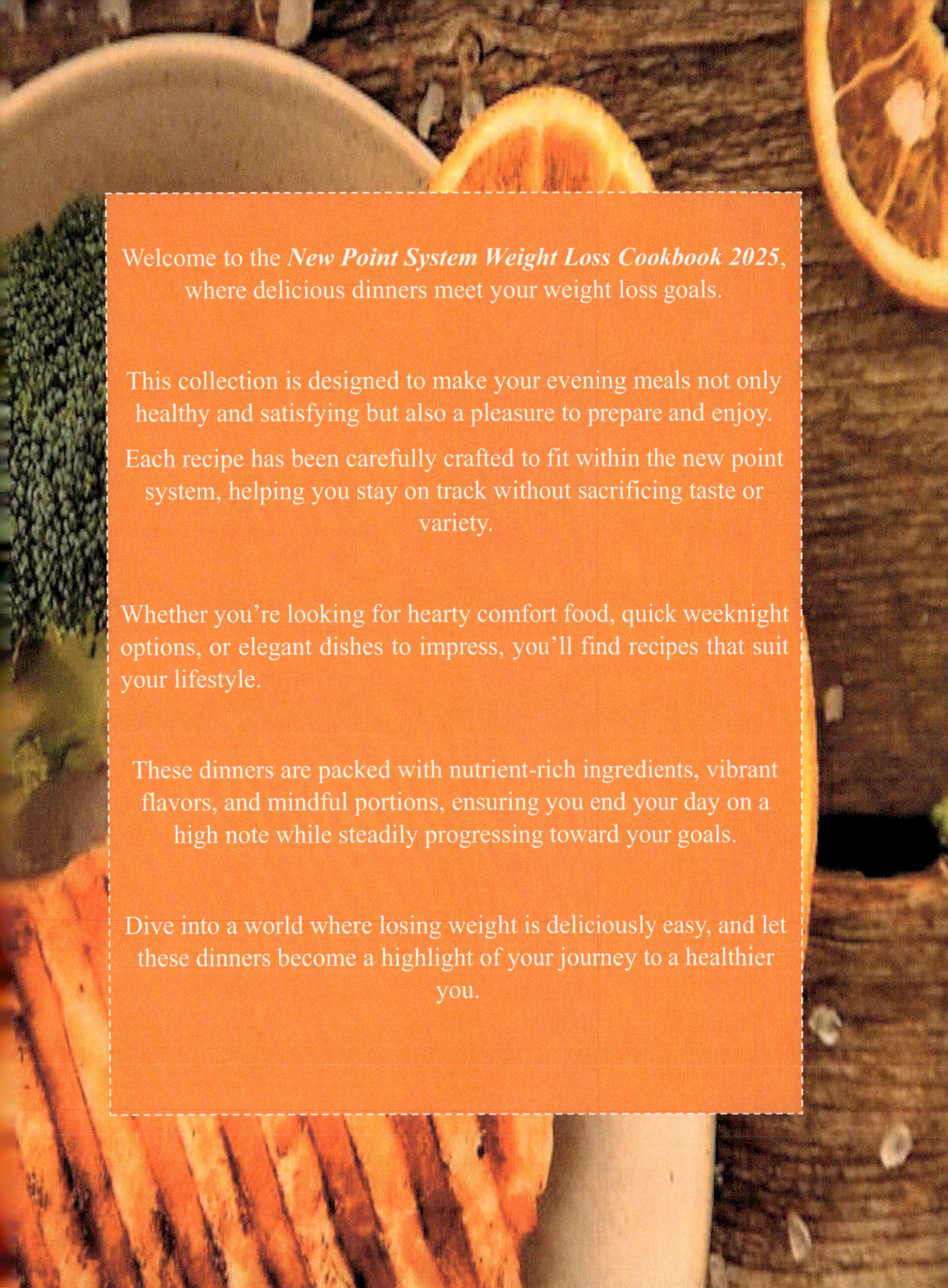

Welcome to the *New Point System Weight Loss Cookbook 2025*, where delicious dinners meet your weight loss goals.

This collection is designed to make your evening meals not only healthy and satisfying but also a pleasure to prepare and enjoy.

Each recipe has been carefully crafted to fit within the new point system, helping you stay on track without sacrificing taste or variety.

Whether you're looking for hearty comfort food, quick weeknight options, or elegant dishes to impress, you'll find recipes that suit your lifestyle.

These dinners are packed with nutrient-rich ingredients, vibrant flavors, and mindful portions, ensuring you end your day on a high note while steadily progressing toward your goals.

Dive into a world where losing weight is deliciously easy, and let these dinners become a highlight of your journey to a healthier you.

- Prep Time: 10 minutes
- Cook Time: 10 minutes
- Total Time: 20 minutes
- Servings: 4
- Point Value: 3 points per serving

LEMON HERB GRILLED SALMON

(4 oz) salmon fillets
2 tbsp olive oil
2 tbsp fresh lemon juice
2 cloves garlic, minced
1 tbsp fresh dill, chopped
1 tbsp fresh parsley, chopped
1 tsp lemon zest
Salt and pepper, to taste

Method:

1 Marinate: In a small bowl, whisk together olive oil, lemon juice, garlic, dill, parsley, lemon zest, salt, and pepper. Place the salmon fillets in a shallow dish and pour the marinade over them. Let it marinate for 10 minutes.

2 Grill: Preheat the grill to medium-high heat. Grill the salmon for 4-5 minutes on each side, until the fish is opaque and flakes easily with a fork.

3 Serve: Remove from the grill and serve immediately with a sprinkle of fresh herbs.

- Prep Time: 10 minutes
- Cooking Time: 15 minutes
- Total Time: 25 minutes
- Servings: 4
- Point Value: 3 points per serving

CHICKEN STIR-FRY WITH MIXED VEGETABLES

1 lb. (450g) skinless, boneless chicken breast, thinly sliced
2 cups broccoli florets
1 red bell pepper, sliced
1 yellow bell pepper, sliced
1 medium carrot, julienned
1 cup snap peas
2 cloves garlic, minced
1 tbsp low-sodium soy sauce
1 tbsp oyster sauce
1 tbsp olive oil
1 tsp sesame oil
1 tsp cornstarch mixed with 2 tbsp water (optional, for thickening)
Salt and pepper to taste

Method:

1. Prepare the Chicken: Season the chicken slices with salt and pepper.
2. Cook the Chicken: In a large skillet or wok, heat the olive oil over medium-high heat. Add the chicken and stir-fry for 5-7 minutes until cooked through. Remove and set aside.
3. Cook the Vegetables: In the same skillet, add a little more oil if needed. Stir-fry the garlic for 30 seconds until fragrant, then add the broccoli, bell peppers, carrot, and snap peas. Cook for 5-7 minutes, until vegetables are tender-crisp.
4. Combine: Return the chicken to the skillet. Add the soy sauce, oyster sauce, and sesame oil. Stir well to combine. If using cornstarch, add the mixture to thicken the sauce.
5. Serve: Divide into four servings and enjoy.

- Prep Time: 10 minutes
- Cook Time: 40 minutes
- Total Time: 50 minutes
- Servings: 4
- Point Value: 3 points per serving

STUFFED BELL PEPPERS WITH GROUND TURKEY

large bell peppers, tops cut off and seeds removed
1 lb. lean ground turkey (93% lean)
1 cup cooked quinoa
½ cup diced onion
½ cup diced tomatoes (canned or fresh)
1/4 cup shredded low-fat mozzarella cheese
2 cloves garlic, minced
1 tsp olive oil
Salt and pepper to taste
Fresh parsley, chopped (for garnish)

Method:

1   Preheat Oven: Preheat the oven to 375°F (190°C).
2   Sauté Turkey: In a large skillet, heat olive oil over medium heat. Add garlic and onion, cooking until soft. Add ground turkey, cooking until browned. Season with salt and pepper.
3   Mix Filling: Stir in quinoa and diced tomatoes. Simmer for 5 minutes.
4   Stuff Peppers: Spoon the turkey mixture into each bell pepper, filling them to the top. Place in a baking dish.
5   Bake: Cover with foil and bake for 30 minutes. Remove foil, sprinkle mozzarella cheese on top, and bake for an additional 10 minutes until cheese melts.
6   Garnish and Serve: Remove from the oven, garnish with parsley, and serve hot.

ZUCCHINI NOODLES WITH MARINARA SAUCE

- Prep Time: 10 minutes
- Cook Time: 10 minutes
- Total Time: 20 minutes
- Servings: 2
- Point Value: 2 points per serving

2 medium zucchinis (spiralized)
1 cup marinara sauce (low-sugar, no-oil added)
1 tsp olive oil
Salt and pepper to taste
1 tbsp grated Parmesan (optional)

Method:

1   Heat olive oil in a large pan over medium heat.
2   Add zucchini noodles and sauté for 2-3 minutes until tender.
3   Heat marinara sauce in a small pot until warmed through.
4   Combine zucchini noodles with marinara sauce, stirring gently.
5   Season with salt and pepper, garnish with Parmesan if desired. Serve immediately.

- Prep Time: 10 mins
- Cook Time: 20 mins
- Total Time: 30 mins
- Servings: 4
- Point Value: 2 points per serving

BAKED COD WITH ROASTED ASPARAGUS

cod fillets (4 oz each)
1 lb. asparagus, trimmed
1 tbsp olive oil
1 lemon, sliced
2 garlic cloves, minced
Salt and pepper to taste
1 tsp paprika

Method:

1 Preheat oven to 400°F (200°C).
2 Place cod fillets on a baking sheet lined with parchment paper. Drizzle with half the olive oil, sprinkle with paprika, salt, and pepper. Add lemon slices on top.
3 Arrange asparagus on a separate sheet pan, drizzle with remaining olive oil, add garlic, salt, and pepper. Toss to coat.
4 Roast cod and asparagus in the oven for 15-20 minutes, until the cod is flaky and asparagus is tender.
5 Serve immediately.

4

Snacks & Light Bites

Snacking is often seen as a guilty pleasure, but in the *New Point System Weight Loss Cookbook 2025*, we redefine it as a vital part of your weight loss journey.

In this section, you'll discover a variety of delicious, satisfying, and low-point snacks and light bites that will keep your energy levels up without sabotaging your progress.

Snacking can be one of the trickiest parts of weight loss—too often, we reach for quick, unhealthy options that derail our progress. But with the right recipes, snacks can actually support your weight loss journey. In this section of the *New Point System Weight Loss Cookbook 2025*, we focus on light bites that are not only delicious but also designed to help you stay on track. We've carefully crafted each snack with nutrient-dense ingredients that satisfy cravings while keeping points low.

From crunchy vegetable crisps and protein-packed dips to refreshing smoothies and energy bites, each recipe prioritizes flavor and convenience. We've also included easy-to-follow point values so you can confidently enjoy your snacks while sticking to your plan. Snack smarter and savor every bite with recipes that align with your healthy lifestyle!

Whether you need a quick mid-morning boost, a post-workout nibble, or a light evening snack, our recipes are designed to fit seamlessly into your day while staying mindful of your goals.

These snacks are simple to prepare, full of flavor, and crafted with the perfect balance of nutrients to keep you satisfied between meals. Welcome to snacking that supports your success!

- Prep Time: 5 minutes
- Cooking Time: 0 minutes
- Total Time: 5 minutes
- Servings: 1
- Point Value: 3 points

APPLE SLICES WITH ALMOND BUTTER

1 medium apple (0 points)
1 tablespoon almond butter (3 points)

Method:

1 Core and slice the apple into thin wedges.
2 Spread 1 tablespoon of almond butter evenly across the apple slices.
3 Serve immediately.

VEGGIE STICKS WITH HUMMUS

- Prep Time: 10 mins
- Cooking Time: None
- Total Time: 10 mins
- Servings: 4
- Point Value: 2 points per serving

1 cup hummus (store-bought or homemade)
2 medium carrots, cut into sticks
2 medium celery stalks, cut into sticks
1 cucumber, cut into sticks
1 red bell pepper, cut into strips

Method:

1 Prepare Veggies: Wash and slice the carrots, celery, cucumber, and bell pepper into sticks.
2 Portion Hummus: Divide the hummus equally into 4 servings, about ¼ cup per portion.
3 Serve: Arrange the veggie sticks on a plate and serve with the hummus for dipping.

- Prep Time: 5 minutes
- Cooking Time: 0 minutes
- Total Time: 5 minutes
- Servings: 1
- Point Value: 4 Points

GREEK YOGURT WITH HONEY AND ALMONDS

½ cup plain non-fat Greek yogurt (0 Points)
1 tsp honey (1 Point)
1 tbsp sliced almonds (3 Points)

Method:

1 Spoon the Greek yogurt into a bowl.
2 Drizzle honey over the top.
3 Sprinkle sliced almonds evenly.
4 Serve immediately and enjoy!

- Prep Time: 5 minutes
- Cook Time: 0 minutes
- Total Time: 5 minutes
- Servings: 8
- Point Value: 6 points per serving

HOMEMADE TRAIL MIX WITH NUTS AND DRIED FRUIT

½ cup almonds (unsalted)
½ cup walnuts (unsalted)
1/4 cup sunflower seeds
1/4 cup pumpkin seeds
½ cup dried cranberries (unsweetened)
½ cup dried apricots (chopped)
1/4 cup dark chocolate chips (70% cacao)

Method:

1   In a large bowl, mix almonds, walnuts, sunflower seeds, and pumpkin seeds.
2   Add dried cranberries, chopped apricots, and dark chocolate chips.
3   Stir until all ingredients are well combined.
4   Store in an airtight container.

- Prep Time: 10 minutes
- Cooking Time: 0 minutes
- Total Time: 10 minutes
- Servings: 4
- Point Value: 2 points per serving

CUCUMBER AND TOMATO SALAD WITH BALSAMIC VINEGAR

2 medium cucumbers, sliced (0 points)
2 medium tomatoes, diced (0 points)
1 tbsp balsamic vinegar (1 point)
1 tbsp olive oil (4 points)
Salt and pepper to taste (0 points)
Fresh basil, chopped (optional, 0 points)

Method:

1 In a large bowl, combine sliced cucumbers and diced tomatoes.
2 Drizzle with balsamic vinegar and olive oil.
3 Season with salt and pepper.
4 Toss gently to coat. Garnish with fresh basil if desired.

5
DESSERTS

In the *New Point System Weight Loss Cookbook 2025*, desserts don't have to be off-limits! With smart ingredients and clever portioning, you can indulge in your favorite sweet treats without derailing your weight loss goals. From lightened-up classics to inventive new creations, this section is packed with delicious, guilt-free options that satisfy your sweet tooth while keeping points in check.

By using lower-calorie swaps, natural sweeteners, and portion-controlled servings, you'll find that each recipe offers a delightful balance of flavor and nutrition. No more sacrificing your cravings – these desserts fit seamlessly into your weight loss plan while making sure you still enjoy the sweet moments of life.

From quick no-bake options to baked favorites, this section proves that you don't need to deprive yourself to succeed. With each recipe, you'll learn how to satisfy your sweet tooth while keeping points in check, so you can celebrate your progress without worry. Here's to treating yourself in a way that supports your goals and keeps the joy of dessert alive!

Whether you crave something fruity, creamy, or chocolaty, these recipes prove that dessert can still be a delightful part of your journey toward a healthier you. Enjoy the sweetness of success, one bite at a time!

- Prep Time: 10 minutes
- Cooking Time: 25 minutes
- Total Time: 35 minutes
- Servings: 4
- Point Value: 2 points per serving

BAKED APPLES WITH CINNAMON

medium apples, cored
1 tsp cinnamon
1 tbsp honey
1 tbsp water
1 tbsp raisins (optional)

Method:

1 Preheat oven to 350°F (175°C).
2 Place cored apples in a baking dish.
3 Mix cinnamon, honey, and water, then drizzle over apples.
4 Add raisins if using.
5 Bake for 25 minutes until apples are tender.
6 Serve warm.

CHOCOLATE CHIA PUDDING

- Prep Time: 5 minutes
- Cooking Time: 0 minutes
- Total Time: 4 hours (chill time)
- Servings: 4
- Point Value: 4 points per serving

1/4 cup chia seeds (4 points)
2 tbsp unsweetened cocoa powder (0 points)
1 ½ cups unsweetened almond milk (1 point)
1 tbsp maple syrup (3 points)
½ tsp vanilla extract (0 points)

Method:

1 In a mixing bowl, whisk together chia seeds, cocoa powder, almond milk, maple syrup, and vanilla extract.
2 Stir well until combined.
3 Cover and refrigerate for at least 4 hours, or overnight, to allow the chia seeds to absorb the liquid and thicken.
4 Stir again before serving. Enjoy chilled.

- Prep Time: 10 mins
- Freezing Time: 4 hours
- Total Time: 4 hours 10 mins
- Servings: 4
- Point Value: 1 point per serving

BERRY SORBET

cups mixed berries (frozen or fresh)
2 tbsp honey or agave syrup
1 tbsp lemon juice

Method:

1 Blend berries, honey, and lemon juice in a food processor until smooth.
2 Pour the mixture into a container and freeze for 4 hours, stirring every hour to prevent large ice crystals.
3 Serve and enjoy.

- Prep Time: 10 minutes
- Chill Time: 4 hours
- Total Time: 4 hours 10 minutes
- Servings: 4
- Point Value: 4 points per serving

MANGO CHIA PUDDING

1 cup unsweetened almond milk
½ cup chia seeds
1 ripe mango, peeled and diced
1 tsp honey

Method:

1. In a medium bowl, whisk together almond milk, chia seeds, and honey.
2. Cover and refrigerate for 4 hours or overnight until the mixture thickens.
3. Once set, stir well, and divide into 4 serving dishes.
4. Top each with diced mango and serve chilled.

- Prep Time: 10 minutes
- Cook Time: 0 minutes
- Total Time: 2 hours (including freezing)
- Servings: 6
- Point Value: 2 points per serving

FROZEN BANANA BITES

2 large bananas
2 tbsp peanut butter (or almond butter)
2 oz dark chocolate (70% cocoa or higher)

Methods:

1. Slice bananas into bite-sized rounds.
2. Spread a small amount of peanut butter between two banana slices to form a sandwich.
3. Melt dark chocolate in the microwave in 30-second intervals, stirring in between until smooth.
4. Dip each banana sandwich into the melted chocolate.
5. Place on a parchment-lined baking sheet and freeze for at least 2 hours.
6. Serve frozen.

6
BEVERAGES

Welcome to the Beverages section of the ***New Point System Weight Loss Cookbook 2025***, where hydration meets flavor without the excess calories. Staying hydrated is essential for both health and weight management, but not all drinks are created equal. In this section, you'll find a collection of refreshing, low-point beverages designed to quench your thirst while keeping you on track with your weight loss goals.

From revitalizing smoothies and detoxifying teas to flavorful infused waters, each recipe is carefully crafted to offer maximum taste with minimal points. Whether you're starting your day with a nutrient-packed smoothie or winding down with a calming herbal tea, these beverages will keep you feeling energized and satisfied. With easy-to-follow instructions and precise point calculations, sipping smarter has never been easier.

So, grab your favorite glass and get ready to enjoy beverages that support your journey to a healthier, happier you!

- Prep Time: 5 minutes
- Cook Time: 0 minutes
- Total Time: 5 minutes
- Servings: 4
- Point Value: 0 points

INFUSED WATER WITH CUCUMBER AND MINT

1 medium cucumber, thinly sliced
10 fresh mint leaves
cups water
Ice cubes (optional)

Method:

1 In a large pitcher, combine cucumber slices and mint leaves.
2 Pour in water and stir gently.
3 Refrigerate for at least 1 hour to infuse flavors.
4 Serve chilled, with ice cubes if desired.

- Prep Time: 5 minutes
- Total Time: 5 minutes
- Servings: 1
- Point Value: 2 points

GREEN DETOX SMOOTHIE

1 cup spinach
½ cup unsweetened almond milk
½ banana
1/4 avocado
1/4 cup cucumber
1 tsp chia seeds
½ cup ice

Method:

1	Combine all ingredients in a blender.
2	Blend until smooth and creamy.
3	Pour into a glass and serve immediately.

- Prep Time: 5 minutes
- Cooking Time: 0 minutes
- Total Time: 5 minutes
- Servings: 4
- Point Value: 0 points per serving

CITRUS REFRESHER WITH LEMON AND ORANGE

- 2 lemons, juiced
- 2 oranges, juiced
- cups cold water
- Ice cubes
- Fresh mint leaves (optional for garnish)

Method:

1 In a large pitcher, combine lemon juice, orange juice, and cold water. Stir well.
2 Fill glasses with ice cubes and pour the citrus mixture over the ice.
3 Garnish with fresh mint leaves if desired.
4 Serve immediately.

SPICED HERBAL TEA

cups water
2 cinnamon sticks
whole cloves
slices fresh ginger
1 star anise
herbal tea bags (e.g., chamomile or peppermint)

- Prep Time: 5 minutes
- Cook Time: 10 minutes
- Total Time: 15 minutes
- Servings: 4
- Point Value: 0 points per serving

Method:

1 In a pot, bring water, cinnamon sticks, cloves, ginger, and star anise to a boil.
2 Reduce heat and simmer for 10 minutes.
3 Remove from heat, add herbal tea bags, and steep for 5 minutes.
4 Strain and serve hot.

- Prep Time: 5 minutes
- Cook Time: 2 minutes
- Total Time: 7 minutes
- Servings: 1
- Point Value: 2 points

MATCHA GREEN TEA LATTE

1 tsp matcha green tea powder (0 points)
½ cup hot water (0 points)
½ cup unsweetened almond milk (1 point)
1 tsp honey or agave syrup (1 point)
Optional: ice for iced latte

Method:

1　Whisk matcha powder with hot water until smooth.
2　Heat almond milk until warm and frothy (or use cold milk for iced latte).
3　Stir in honey or agave.
4　Combine matcha mixture with almond milk.
5　Serve warm or over ice.

7
SOUP

Welcome to the Soups section of the *New Point System Weight Loss Cookbook 2025*, where warmth meets nourishment. Soups are a versatile and satisfying option for any meal, whether you're looking for a light starter or a hearty main course.

Packed with fresh vegetables, lean proteins, and flavorful herbs and spices, these recipes are designed to fuel your body while helping you stay on track with your weight loss goals.

Each soup is carefully portioned and aligned with the new point system, allowing you to enjoy delicious meals without the guesswork.

From creamy bisques to brothy vegetable soups, this section offers a variety of choices that will warm your soul and keep your diet in check. Let these recipes show you how simple ingredients can come together to create meals that are as comforting as they are healthy.

So grab a spoon, and let's dive into the world of flavorful, nutritious soups that will help you savor every bite on your weight loss journey!

- Prep Time: 10 minutes
- Cook Time: 25 minutes
- Total Time: 35 minutes
- Servings: 4
- Point Value: 3 points per serving

BUTTERNUT SQUASH SOUP WITH COCONUT MILK

1 medium butternut squash, peeled and cubed
1 can (14 oz) light coconut milk
1 small onion, diced
2 cloves garlic, minced
1 tsp olive oil
2 cups vegetable broth
Salt and pepper to taste
Optional: Fresh cilantro for garnish

Method:

1. In a large pot, heat olive oil over medium heat. Sauté onion and garlic until softened, about 5 minutes.
2. Add cubed butternut squash and vegetable broth. Bring to a boil, then reduce heat and simmer for 20 minutes, until squash is tender.
3. Stir in coconut milk, season with salt and pepper. Blend soup with an immersion blender until smooth.
4. Serve hot, garnished with fresh cilantro if desired.

- Prep Time: 15 mins
- Cook Time: 30 mins
- Total Time: 45 mins
- Servings: 4
- Point Value: 3 per serving

CHICKEN AND VEGETABLE SOUP WITH QUINOA

1 lb. boneless, skinless chicken breast, diced
½ cup quinoa, rinsed
1 onion, diced
2 carrots, sliced
2 celery stalks, chopped
cups low-sodium chicken broth
1 zucchini, diced
1 cup spinach, chopped
2 garlic cloves, minced
1 tsp olive oil
Salt and pepper to taste
Fresh parsley for garnish (optional)

Method:

1 Heat olive oil in a large pot over medium heat. Sauté onions, carrots, celery, and garlic for 5 minutes.
2 Add chicken and cook until browned, about 5 minutes.
3 Stir in quinoa and chicken broth. Bring to a boil, reduce heat, and simmer for 20 minutes.
4 Add zucchini and spinach. Cook for an additional 5 minutes.
5 Season with salt and pepper. Garnish with parsley and serve hot.

- Prep Time: 10 minutes
- Cook Time: 30 minutes
- Total Time: 40 minutes
- Servings: 4
- Point Value: 2 points per serving

SPICY BLACK BEAN SOUP WITH CILANTRO

2 cans (15 oz each) black beans, drained and rinsed
1 tbsp olive oil
1 small onion, diced
garlic cloves, minced
1 tsp ground cumin
1 tsp chili powder
1/4 tsp cayenne pepper (optional, for extra heat)
cups low-sodium vegetable broth
Juice of 1 lime
1/4 cup fresh cilantro, chopped
Salt and pepper to taste

Method:

1. Heat olive oil in a pot over medium heat. Sauté onions until soft (about 5 minutes).
2. Add garlic, cumin, chili powder, and cayenne pepper; cook for 1 minute.
3. Stir in black beans and vegetable broth. Bring to a boil, then reduce heat and simmer for 20 minutes.
4. Remove from heat, blend half the soup for a creamy texture.
5. Stir in lime juice and chopped cilantro. Adjust seasoning with salt and pepper.
6. Serve hot, garnished with additional cilantro if desired.

- Prep Time: 10 minutes
- Cook Time: 25 minutes
- Total Time: 35 minutes
- Servings: 4
- Point Value: 2 points per serving

TOMATO BASIL SOUP WITH GREEK YOGURT

1 tbsp olive oil (4 points)
1 small onion, diced
2 garlic cloves, minced
cups diced tomatoes (fresh or canned)
2 cups vegetable broth
1/4 cup fresh basil leaves
½ cup plain non-fat Greek yogurt (0 points)
Salt and pepper to taste

Methods:

1 Heat olive oil in a pot over medium heat. Add onion and garlic, sauté until soft (about 5 minutes).
2 Add diced tomatoes and vegetable broth. Simmer for 20 minutes.
3 Stir in fresh basil, then remove from heat.
4 Blend the soup until smooth using an immersion blender or regular blender.
5 Stir in Greek yogurt, season with salt and pepper, and serve warm.

- Prep Time: 10 minutes
- Cook Time: 25 minutes
- Total Time: 35 minutes
- Servings: 4
- Point Value: 2 points per serving

CARROT GINGER SOUP WITH LIME

1 lb. carrots, peeled and chopped
1 tbsp olive oil (3 points)
1 small onion, chopped
2-inch piece fresh ginger, grated
cups vegetable broth, low-sodium
Juice of 1 lime
Salt and pepper to taste

Method:

1 Heat olive oil in a pot over medium heat. Sauté onions and ginger until softened, about 5 minutes.
2 Add carrots and vegetable broth. Bring to a boil, then reduce heat and simmer for 20 minutes until carrots are tender.
3 Blend the soup until smooth. Stir in lime juice and season with salt and pepper.
4 Serve hot.

8
VEGETABLES

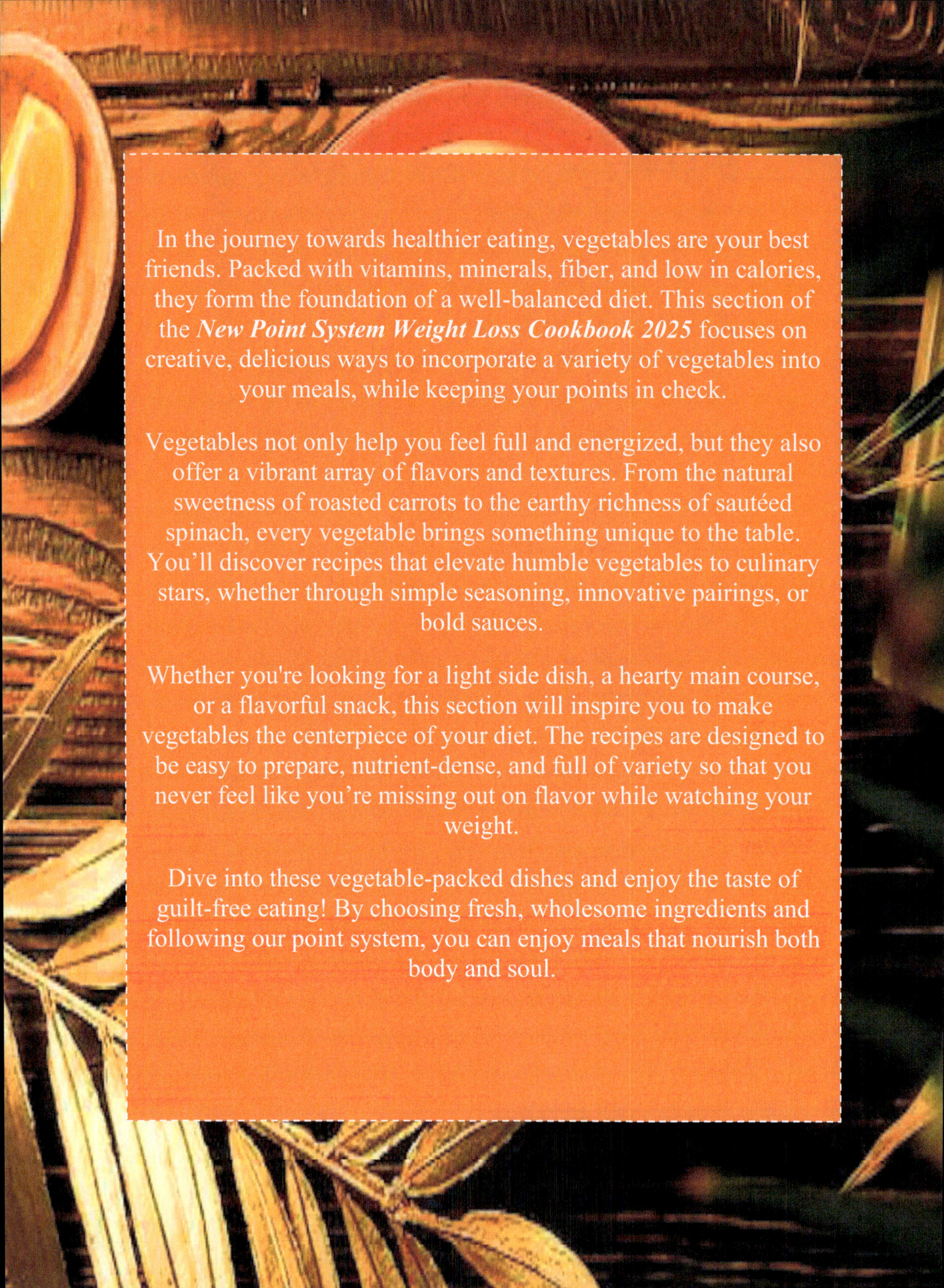

In the journey towards healthier eating, vegetables are your best friends. Packed with vitamins, minerals, fiber, and low in calories, they form the foundation of a well-balanced diet. This section of the ***New Point System Weight Loss Cookbook 2025*** focuses on creative, delicious ways to incorporate a variety of vegetables into your meals, while keeping your points in check.

Vegetables not only help you feel full and energized, but they also offer a vibrant array of flavors and textures. From the natural sweetness of roasted carrots to the earthy richness of sautéed spinach, every vegetable brings something unique to the table. You'll discover recipes that elevate humble vegetables to culinary stars, whether through simple seasoning, innovative pairings, or bold sauces.

Whether you're looking for a light side dish, a hearty main course, or a flavorful snack, this section will inspire you to make vegetables the centerpiece of your diet. The recipes are designed to be easy to prepare, nutrient-dense, and full of variety so that you never feel like you're missing out on flavor while watching your weight.

Dive into these vegetable-packed dishes and enjoy the taste of guilt-free eating! By choosing fresh, wholesome ingredients and following our point system, you can enjoy meals that nourish both body and soul.

- Prep Time: 10 mins
- Cook Time: 25 mins
- Total Time: 35 mins
- Servings: 4
- Point Value: 2 points per serving

ROASTED BRUSSELS SPROUTS WITH BALSAMIC GLAZE

1 lb. Brussels sprouts, halved
1 tbsp olive oil
1 tbsp balsamic vinegar
1 tsp honey
Salt and pepper to taste

Method:

1	Preheat oven to 400°F (200°C).
2	Toss Brussels sprouts with olive oil, salt, and pepper.
3	Spread on a baking sheet in a single layer and roast for 20-25 minutes until tender and caramelized.
4	In a small bowl, mix balsamic vinegar and honey.
5	Drizzle the glaze over the roasted Brussels sprouts before serving.

- Prep Time: 5 minutes
- Cook Time: 5 minutes
- Total Time: 10 minutes
- Servings: 4
- Point Value: 1 per serving

SAUTÉED SPINACH WITH GARLIC AND LEMON

1 lb. fresh spinach
2 tsp olive oil
garlic cloves, minced
Juice of 1 lemon
Salt and pepper to taste

Method:

1 Heat olive oil in a large skillet over medium heat.
2 Add minced garlic and sauté for 1 minute until fragrant.
3 Add spinach to the skillet and cook, stirring occasionally, until wilted, about 3-4 minutes.
4 Squeeze lemon juice over the spinach and season with salt and pepper.
5 Serve immediately.

- Prep Time: 5 minutes
- Cook Time: 10 minutes
- Total Time: 15 minutes
- Servings: 4
- Point Value: 2 points per serving

GRILLED ZUCCHINI WITH PARMESAN

medium zucchinis, sliced lengthwise
1 tbsp olive oil
¼ cup grated Parmesan cheese
Salt and pepper to taste

Method:

- Preheat the grill to medium heat.
- Brush zucchini slices with olive oil and season with salt and pepper.
- Grill zucchini for 3-4 minutes on each side, until tender and lightly charred.
- Sprinkle with Parmesan cheese immediately after grilling.
- Serve warm.

- Prep Time: 5 minutes
- Cook Time: 5 minutes
- Total Time: 10 minutes
- Servings: 4
- Point Value: 2 points per serving

STEAMED BROCCOLI WITH OLIVE OIL AND LEMON

cups broccoli florets
1 tbsp olive oil (3 points)
Juice of 1 lemon
Salt and pepper, to taste

Method:

1. Steam broccoli for 5 minutes until tender yet crisp.
2. Drizzle with olive oil and lemon juice.
3. Season with salt and pepper.
4. Toss and serve immediately.

- Prep Time: 10 minutes
- Cook Time: 10 minutes
- Total Time: 20 minutes
- Servings: 4
- Point Value: 2 points per serving

CAULIFLOWER RICE STIR-FRY WITH SOY SAUCE

cups cauliflower rice
1 tbsp olive oil
1 small onion, diced
1 red bell pepper, diced
1 carrot, shredded
2 tbsp low-sodium soy sauce
1 tsp garlic powder
1 tsp ginger powder
1/4 cup green onions, chopped (optional)

Method:

1 Heat olive oil in a large pan over medium heat.
2 Sauté onions, bell pepper, and carrot for 5 minutes until softened.
3 Add cauliflower rice, garlic powder, and ginger powder; stir-fry for 3-4 minutes.
4 Pour in soy sauce and cook for another 2 minutes until well combined.
5 Garnish with green onions if desired. Serve warm.

9
BEEF

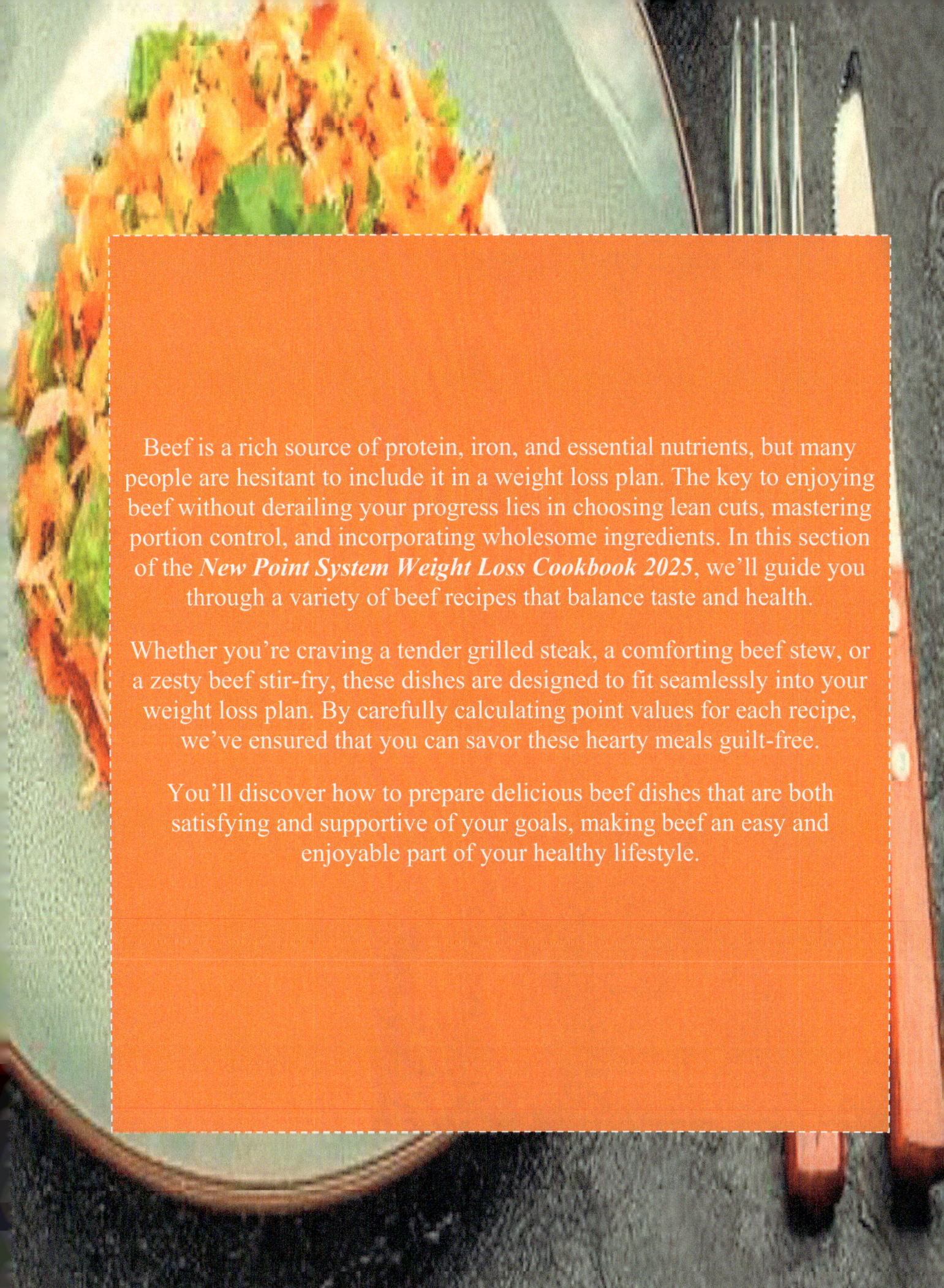

Beef is a rich source of protein, iron, and essential nutrients, but many people are hesitant to include it in a weight loss plan. The key to enjoying beef without derailing your progress lies in choosing lean cuts, mastering portion control, and incorporating wholesome ingredients. In this section of the *New Point System Weight Loss Cookbook 2025*, we'll guide you through a variety of beef recipes that balance taste and health.

Whether you're craving a tender grilled steak, a comforting beef stew, or a zesty beef stir-fry, these dishes are designed to fit seamlessly into your weight loss plan. By carefully calculating point values for each recipe, we've ensured that you can savor these hearty meals guilt-free.

You'll discover how to prepare delicious beef dishes that are both satisfying and supportive of your goals, making beef an easy and enjoyable part of your healthy lifestyle.

- Prep Time: 10 minutes
- Cook Time: 15 minutes
- Total Time: 25 minutes
- Servings: 4
- Point Value: 6 points per serving

LEAN BEEF STIR-FRY WITH VEGETABLES

12 oz lean beef sirloin, sliced thin
1 tbsp olive oil
1 red bell pepper, sliced
1 zucchini, sliced
1 carrot, sliced
1 cup broccoli florets
2 tbsp low-sodium soy sauce
1 tsp grated ginger
1 garlic clove, minced

Method:

1   Heat 1 tbsp olive oil in a large skillet over medium-high heat.
2   Add beef and stir-fry for 5 minutes until browned.
3   Add garlic and ginger; cook for 1 minute.
4   Add vegetables and stir-fry for 7-8 minutes until tender-crisp.
5   Stir in soy sauce and cook for 2 minutes.
6   Serve hot.

- Prep Time: 20 minutes
- Cook Time: 40 minutes
- Total Time: 1 hour
- Servings: 4
- Point Value per Serving: 6 points

BEEF AND CABBAGE ROLL-UPS WITH TOMATO SAUCE

large cabbage leaves
1 lb. lean ground beef (96% lean)
½ cup cooked brown rice
1 small onion, finely chopped
2 garlic cloves, minced
1 tsp paprika
Salt and pepper to taste
2 cups tomato sauce (low sodium)
1 tbsp olive oil

Method:

1. Preheat oven to 350°F (175°C).
2. Blanch cabbage leaves in boiling water for 2-3 minutes, until softened. Drain and set aside.
3. In a bowl, mix ground beef, cooked rice, onion, garlic, paprika, salt, and pepper.
4. Place a portion of the beef mixture onto each cabbage leaf, roll up, and secure with toothpicks.
5. In a large skillet, heat olive oil over medium heat and sear the roll-ups on all sides.
6. Pour tomato sauce over the roll-ups, cover, and bake in the oven for 30 minutes.
7. Serve warm with extra sauce spooned over the top.

- Prep Time: 15 minutes
- Cook Time: 10 minutes
- Total Time: 25 minutes
- Servings: 4
- Point Value per Serving: 7 points

GRILLED STEAK SALAD WITH MIXED GREENS AND BALSAMIC DRESSING

12 oz lean sirloin steak, trimmed of fat
cups mixed greens
1 cup cherry tomatoes, halved
1/4 cup red onion, thinly sliced
1/4 cup crumbled feta cheese
2 tbsp balsamic vinegar
1 tbsp olive oil
Salt and pepper to taste

Method:

1 Preheat grill to medium-high heat.
2 Season steak with salt and pepper, and grill for 4-5 minutes per side for medium-rare. Let rest, then slice thinly.
3 In a large bowl, toss mixed greens, cherry tomatoes, and red onion.
4 Whisk balsamic vinegar and olive oil together for the dressing.
5 Top salad with steak slices, feta, and drizzle with dressing.
6 Serve immediately.

- Prep Time: 15 minutes
- Cook Time: 6 Hours
- Total Time: 6 hours
- Servings: 6
- Point Value: 5 points per serving

SLOW-COOKED BEEF AND VEGETABLE STEW

1 lb. lean beef stew meat
carrots, chopped
2 celery stalks, chopped
1 onion, chopped
potatoes, cubed
2 cups low-sodium beef broth
1 can diced tomatoes (no added salt)
2 garlic cloves, minced
1 tsp thyme
1 tsp rosemary
Salt and pepper to taste

Method:

1 Add all ingredients to a slow cooker.
2 Cook on low for 6-8 hours or until beef is tender.
3 Adjust seasoning and serve warm.

- Prep Time: 10 mins
- Cook Time: 20 mins
- Total Time: 30 mins
- Servings: 4
- Point Value: 5 points per serving

GROUND BEEF STUFFED PORTOBELLO MUSHROOMS

large Portobello mushrooms
oz lean ground beef (93% lean)
1 small onion, diced
1 garlic clove, minced
1/4 cup grated Parmesan cheese
1/4 tsp salt
1/4 tsp black pepper
1 tbsp olive oil
1/4 cup chopped parsley (optional for garnish)

Method:

1. Preheat oven to 375°F (190°C).
2. Clean mushrooms and remove stems.
3. Heat olive oil in a skillet over medium heat. Cook onions and garlic until softened.
4. Add ground beef, salt, and pepper. Cook until beef is browned, about 5-7 minutes.
5. Stir in Parmesan cheese.
6. Stuff each mushroom cap with the beef mixture.
7. Place mushrooms on a baking sheet and bake for 15 minutes, until tender.
8. Garnish with parsley and serve.

10
PORK

Pork, often regarded as the "**other white meat**," is a flavorful and versatile protein that can be seamlessly integrated into a balanced and health-conscious diet. While some cuts of pork are higher in fat, there are plenty of lean options that provide essential nutrients without tipping the scale. In the *New Point System Weight Loss Cookbook 2025*, we've carefully crafted a collection of pork recipes that not only satisfy your taste buds but also help you stay on track with your weight loss journey.

When choosing pork for your meals, it's essential to focus on lean cuts, such as tenderloin, pork loin chops, and certain cuts from the leg. These options are lower in saturated fat and calories while still providing a rich source of protein, iron, and B vitamins that are crucial for maintaining energy levels and promoting muscle repair.

This section of the cookbook highlights recipes that make the most of these lean cuts, ensuring that every bite is as nutritious as it is delicious.

What sets pork apart from other proteins is its incredible versatility. It can be grilled, roasted, stir-fried, or slow-cooked, and it pairs beautifully with a wide range of spices, herbs, and marinades.

The recipes featured in this section embrace that versatility, offering you an exciting array of flavors and cooking techniques. From savory roasted pork tenderloin with herbs to a spicy pork stir-fry with vegetables, these dishes are designed to keep your meals interesting while adhering to the principles of weight loss and healthy eating.

- Prep Time: 10 mins
- Cook Time: 20 mins
- Total Time: 30 mins
- Servings: 4
- Point Value: 5 points per serving

GRILLED PORK TENDERLOIN WITH APPLE SLICES

1 lb. pork tenderloin (trimmed of fat)
2 medium apples, sliced
1 tbsp olive oil
1 tsp cinnamon
1 tsp garlic powder
Salt and pepper to taste

Method:

1 Preheat grill to medium-high heat.
2 Rub pork tenderloin with olive oil, garlic powder, salt, and pepper.
3 Grill pork for 15-20 minutes, turning occasionally, until internal temperature reaches 145°F.
4 Grill apple slices for 3-5 minutes until tender and slightly charred.
5 Let pork rest for 5 minutes, then slice and serve with grilled apples.

- Prep Time: 10 minutes
- Cook Time: 25 minutes
- Total Time: 35 minutes
- Servings: 4
- Point Value per Serving: 5

BAKED PORK CHOPS WITH MUSTARD AND HERBS

boneless pork chops (4 oz each)
2 tbsp Dijon mustard
1 tbsp olive oil
2 tsp dried thyme
1 tsp garlic powder
Salt and pepper to taste

Method:

1 Preheat oven to 400°F (200°C).
2 In a bowl, mix mustard, olive oil, thyme, garlic powder, salt, and pepper.
3 Brush mixture onto both sides of the pork chops.
4 Place pork chops on a baking sheet and bake for 25 minutes, or until fully cooked.
5 Serve immediately.

- Prep Time: 10 minutes
- Cook Time: 10 minutes
- Total Time: 20 minutes
- Servings: 4
- Point Value: 6 points per serving

PORK LETTUCE WRAPS WITH HOISIN SAUCE

1 lb. lean ground pork
2 tbsp hoisin sauce
1 tbsp low-sodium soy sauce
1 tbsp rice vinegar
2 garlic cloves, minced
1 tbsp fresh ginger, minced
1 tbsp sesame oil
large lettuce leaves (romaine or butter lettuce)
1/4 cup shredded carrots (optional)
1/4 cup chopped scallions (optional)

Methods:

1   Heat sesame oil in a pan over medium heat. Add garlic and ginger; cook for 1 minute.
2   Add ground pork; cook until browned, about 7-8 minutes.
3   Stir in hoisin sauce, soy sauce, and rice vinegar. Simmer for 2 minutes.
4   Spoon pork mixture into lettuce leaves. Top with shredded carrots and scallions if desired.
5   Serve immediately and enjoy.

- Prep Time: 15 minutes
- Cook Time: 8 hours
- Total Time: 8 hours 15 minutes
- Servings: 6
- Point Value per Serving: 7 points

SLOW-COOKED PULLED PORK WITH CABBAGE SLAW

1 ½ lbs. pork shoulder, trimmed of fat (24 points)
1 tbsp olive oil (4 points)
1 tbsp smoked paprika
1 tsp garlic powder
1 tsp cumin
1 tsp salt
½ tsp black pepper
½ cup low-sugar BBQ sauce (4 points)
cups shredded cabbage
1 medium carrot, shredded
2 tbsp apple cider vinegar
1 tbsp Dijon mustard (0 points)
Salt and pepper to taste

Method:

1   Rub pork shoulder with olive oil, smoked paprika, garlic powder, cumin, salt, and pepper.
2   Place in slow cooker and add BBQ sauce. Cover and cook on low for 8 hours until pork is tender.
3   Shred pork using two forks.
4   In a bowl, combine shredded cabbage, carrot, apple cider vinegar, and mustard. Season with salt and pepper.
5   Serve pulled pork with cabbage slaw on the side.

- Prep Time: 10 mins
- Cooking Time: 15 mins
- Total Time: 25 mins
- Servings: 4
- Point Value: 6 points per serving

STIR-FRIED PORK AND PEPPERS WITH GINGER

1 lb. lean pork tenderloin, thinly sliced
2 red bell peppers, thinly sliced
1 green bell pepper, thinly sliced
1 tbsp fresh ginger, grated
2 garlic cloves, minced
2 tbsp low-sodium soy sauce
1 tbsp sesame oil
1 tbsp olive oil
1 tbsp rice vinegar
1 tsp honey
1/4 tsp red pepper flakes (optional)

Method:

1. Heat olive oil in a large skillet over medium-high heat. Add pork slices and stir-fry for 5-6 minutes until browned and cooked through. Remove and set aside.
2. In the same skillet, add sesame oil. Stir-fry ginger and garlic for 1 minute until fragrant.
3. Add bell peppers and cook for 4-5 minutes until tender-crisp.
4. Return pork to the skillet. Add soy sauce, rice vinegar, honey, and red pepper flakes. Stir and cook for another 2 minutes until well combined.
5. Serve immediately.

11
CONCLUSION

Meal Planning and Prep

Meal planning and preparation is a cornerstone of successful weight loss and maintaining a healthy lifestyle. It provides the structure needed to stay on track, avoid impulsive eating, and make nourishing choices even on the busiest days. With the *New Point System Weight Loss Cookbook 2025*, meal planning and prep will be easier and more effective, helping you reach your weight loss goals while enjoying delicious and satisfying meals.

Why Meal Planning is Essential

The main advantage of meal planning is that it allows you to make conscious, informed decisions about what you eat. By taking time to plan ahead, you can:

1. **Control Portions and Ingredients:** Meal planning enables you to pre-portion your meals, ensuring you stay within your point system target while enjoying balanced, nutrient-dense meals.

2. **Reduce Stress and Save Time:** By having a plan in place, you eliminate the guesswork of what to eat, freeing up time and reducing stress, especially during busy workdays.

3. **Stay Consistent:** When you have healthy meals ready to go, you're less likely to veer off course and grab unhealthy snacks or fast food.

4. **Avoid Food Waste:** Planning helps you buy only what you need, minimizing food waste and making the most of your groceries.

5. **Enhance Accountability:** A structured plan keeps you accountable to your health goals, allowing you to track your progress and adjust as needed.

Steps to Effective Meal Planning

1. **Set Your Weekly Goals:** Begin by defining your point goals for the week. Decide on the balance of meals, snacks, and desserts that will help you stay within your desired daily point allowance.

2. **Choose Your Recipes:** Select recipes from the cookbook that fit your taste preferences and goals. Variety is important to prevent boredom and to ensure you're getting a wide range of nutrients.

3. **Create a Shopping List:** Once you've chosen your recipes, write down all the ingredients you'll need for the week. Organize the list by categories (e.g., produce, dairy, protein) to make grocery shopping more efficient.

4. **Prep in Batches:** Set aside time on the weekend or during a free day to batch cook and prepare meals. This could include chopping vegetables, pre-cooking proteins, and assembling snacks so everything is ready for the week.

5. **Portion and Store:** Use containers to portion out individual meals according to your point system. Label them with the meal and its point value so you can easily grab what you need. Use freezer-safe containers for meals that you plan to eat later in the week to preserve freshness.

6. **Keep Snacks Handy:** Prep grab-and-go snacks that are within your point system, such as pre-portioned bags of nuts, chopped fruits, or veggie sticks with hummus.

2-Week Meal Plan for New Point System Weight Loss Cookbook 2025

Week 1

Day 1
- **Breakfast:** Berry Power Smoothie
- **Lunch:** Grilled Chicken Salad with Lemon Vinaigrette
- **Dinner:** Lemon Herb Grilled Salmon
- **Snack:** Apple Slices with Almond Butter
- **Dessert:** Baked Apples with Cinnamon
- **Beverage:** Infused Water with Cucumber and Mint

Day 2
- **Breakfast:** Veggie Omelet
- **Lunch:** Quinoa and Black Bean Salad
- **Dinner:** Chicken Stir-Fry with Mixed Vegetables
- **Snack:** Veggie Sticks with Hummus
- **Dessert:** Chocolate Chia Pudding
- **Beverage:** Green Detox Smoothie

Day 3
- **Breakfast:** Overnight Oats with Chia Seeds
- **Lunch:** Turkey and Avocado Lettuce Wraps
- **Dinner:** Stuffed Bell Peppers with Ground Turkey
- **Snack:** Greek Yogurt with Honey and Almonds
- **Dessert:** Berry Sorbet
- **Beverage:** Citrus Refresher with Lemon and Orange

Day 4
- **Breakfast:** Greek Yogurt Parfait with Fresh Fruit
- **Lunch:** Spinach and Feta Stuffed Portobello Mushrooms
- **Dinner:** Zucchini Noodles with Marinara Sauce
- Snack: Homemade Trail Mix with Nuts and Dried Fruit
- **Dessert:** Mango Chia Pudding
- **Beverage:** Spiced Herbal Tea

Day 5
- **Breakfast:** Avocado Toast with Tomato and Basil
- **Lunch:** Tomato Basil Soup
- **Dinner:** Baked Cod with Roasted Asparagus

- Snack: Cucumber and Tomato Salad with Balsamic Vinegar
- **Dessert:** Frozen Banana Bites
- **Beverage:** Matcha Green Tea Latte

Week 2
Day 1
- **Breakfast:** Berry Power Smoothie
- **Lunch:** Grilled Chicken Salad with Lemon Vinaigrette
- **Dinner:** Chicken Stir-Fry with Mixed Vegetables
- **Snack:** Apple Slices with Almond Butter
- **Dessert:** Chocolate Chia Pudding
- **Beverage:** Infused Water with Cucumber and Mint

Day 2
- **Breakfast:** Veggie Omelet
- **Lunch:** Quinoa and Black Bean Salad
- **Dinner:** Lemon Herb Grilled Salmon
- **Snack:** Veggie Sticks with Hummus
- **Dessert:** Berry Sorbet
- **Beverage:** Green Detox Smoothie

Day 3
- **Breakfast:** Overnight Oats with Chia Seeds
- **Lunch:** Turkey and Avocado Lettuce Wraps
- **Dinner:** Stuffed Bell Peppers with Ground Turkey
- **Snack:** Greek Yogurt with Honey and Almonds
- **Dessert:** Baked Apples with Cinnamon
- **Beverage:** Citrus Refresher with Lemon and Orange

Day 4
- **Breakfast:** Greek Yogurt Parfait with Fresh Fruit
- **Lunch:** Spinach and Feta Stuffed Portobello Mushrooms
- **Dinner:** Zucchini Noodles with Marinara Sauce
- **Snack:** Homemade Trail Mix with Nuts and Dried Fruit
- **Dessert:** Mango Chia Pudding
- **Beverage:** Spiced Herbal Tea

Day 5
- **Breakfast:** Avocado Toast with Tomato and Basil
- **Lunch:** Tomato Basil Soup

- **Dinner:** Baked Cod with Roasted Asparagus
- **Snack:** Cucumber and Tomato Salad with Balsamic Vinegar
- **Dessert:** Frozen Banana Bites
- **Beverage:** Matcha Green Tea Latte

Tips for Successful Meal Prep

1. **Start Small:** If you're new to meal planning, start with prepping a few meals or snacks at a time. As you become more comfortable, you can expand to preparing a full week's worth of meals.

2. **Mix and Match:** Prepare versatile ingredients that can be used in multiple dishes. For example, grilled chicken can be added to salads, wraps, or enjoyed with roasted vegetables.

3. **Use Proper Storage:** Invest in quality storage containers that are airtight, stackable, and portion-friendly. Glass containers work well for reheating meals directly.

4. **Embrace Freezer-Friendly Recipes:** Many of the recipes in this cookbook can be frozen, so don't hesitate to double a recipe and store half for later. This is especially useful for soups, stews, and casseroles.

5. **Stay Flexible:** Life happens, and your meal plan might need to adapt. Keep a few quick, low-point options on hand like boiled eggs, Greek yogurt, or pre-cooked vegetables for those days when you need to change things up.

Printed in Great Britain
by Amazon